A Few Things I've Learned About Being a Man

By
Larry Hughes

A Few Things I've Learned About Being a Man

by Larry Hughes

Copyright © Larry Hughes

A Few Things Press

www.AFewThingsPress.com

Printed in the United States of America

First Printing: November 2016

ISBN-10: 0692807500
ISBN-13: 978-0692807507

TO
LAUGHTER

WE'RE ATTRACTED TO YOUR CURVES BECAUSE
THEY SMOOTH OUT OUR ANGLES.

SOME PARTS OF US ARE JUST NOT WIRED TO EVOLVE.

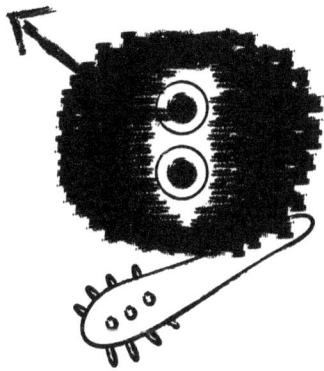

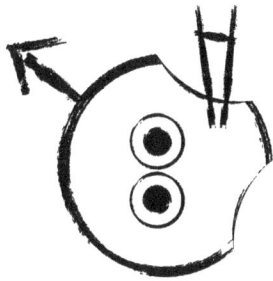

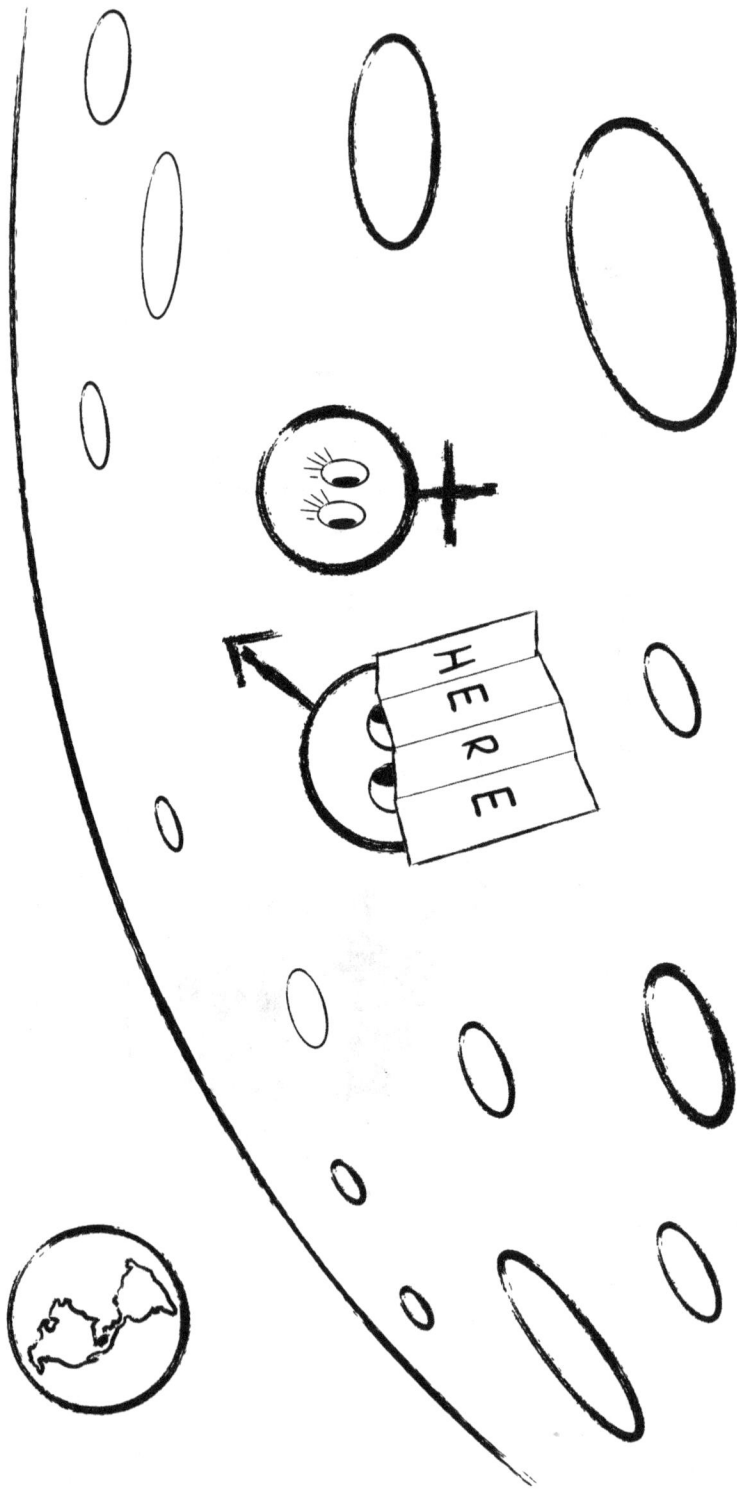

WE DON'T MIND ASKING FOR DIRECTIONS,
IT'S THE ANSWERS WE HATE.

WE SECRETLY IMAGINE OURSELVES AS SUPERHEROES.

To you it's raising kids, to us it's one long playdate.

THE DIFFERENCE WHEN WE MEET OUR FRIENDS
IS ABOUT 5 OCTAVES.

WE'LL SURRENDER OUR MAN CAVES WHEN
YOU SURRENDER THE BATHROOMS.

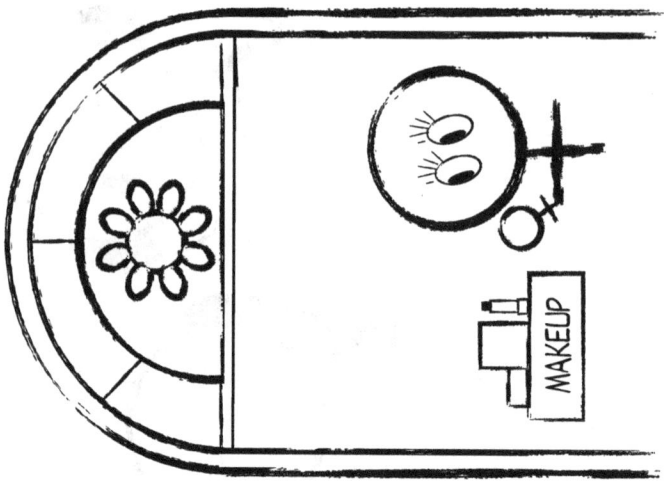

POTTY HUMOR IS THE PRICE OF POTTY DUTY.

IF WE DIDN'T THINK ABOUT IT EVERY 7 SECONDS, WE'D PROBABLY FORGET TO SHOWER.

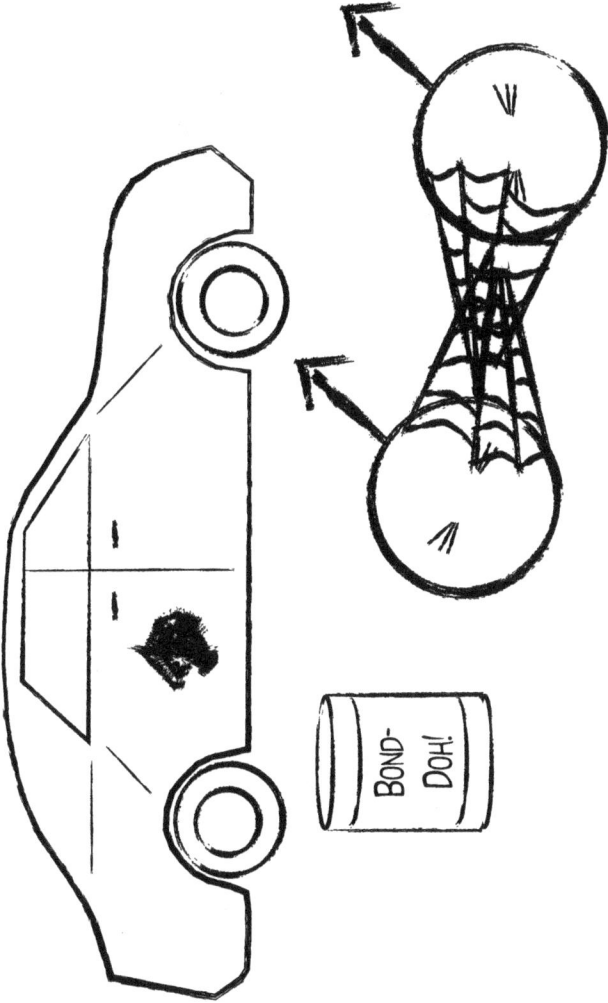

BONDING KEEPS US CLOSE.

SOMETIMES WE'RE A LITTLE TOO COMPETITIVE.

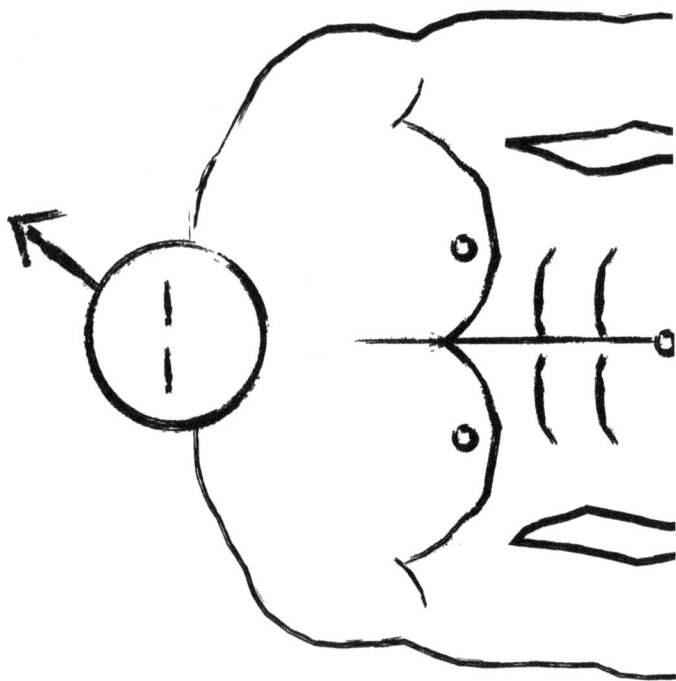

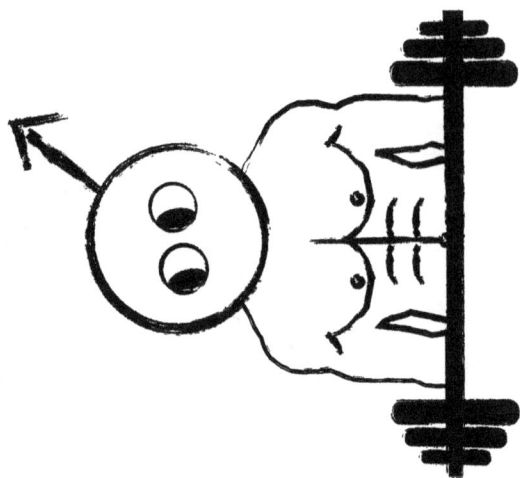

WE ALSO LIKE THE IDEA OF "EQUAL-BUT-DIFFERENT."

WE RESCUE KITTENS EVEN WHEN NOBODY'S THERE TO SEE IT.

THE ACTUAL GIFT IS NOT HAVING TO WRITE A THANK YOU NOTE.

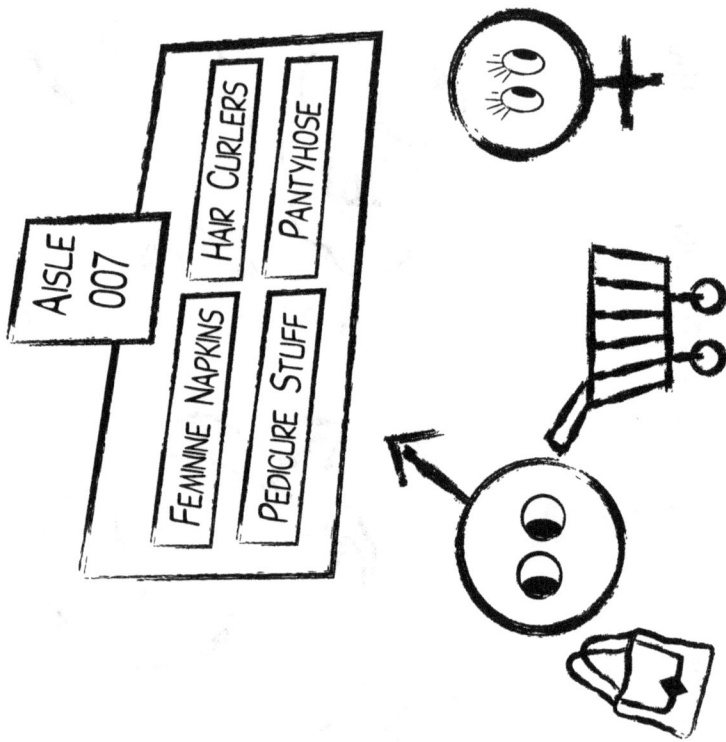

THIS KINDA STUFF NEVER HAPPENS TO JAMES BOND.

AISLE
007

HAIR CURLERS

PANTYHOSE

FEMININE NAPKINS

PEDICURE STUFF

WE CONFRONT OUR MORTALITY THE FIRST TIME
WE HOLD OUR CHILDREN.

IT'S HARD TO PASS UP A GOOD DEAL AT THE HARDWARE STORE.

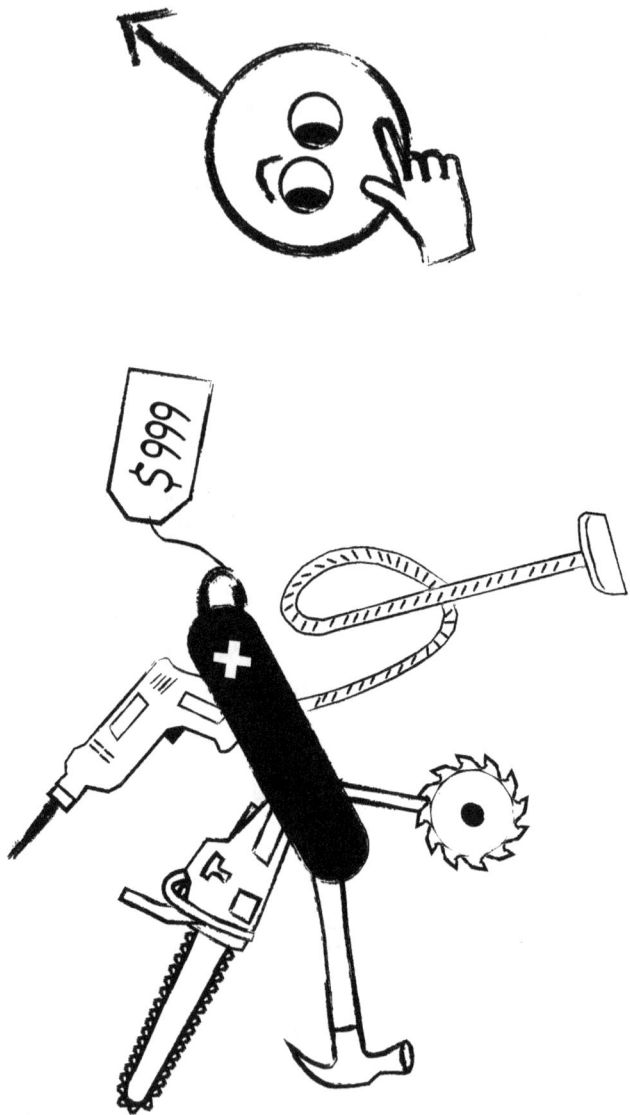

THOSE COLLEGE MEMORIES OF OURSELVES ARE PRETTY UNBELIEVABLE.

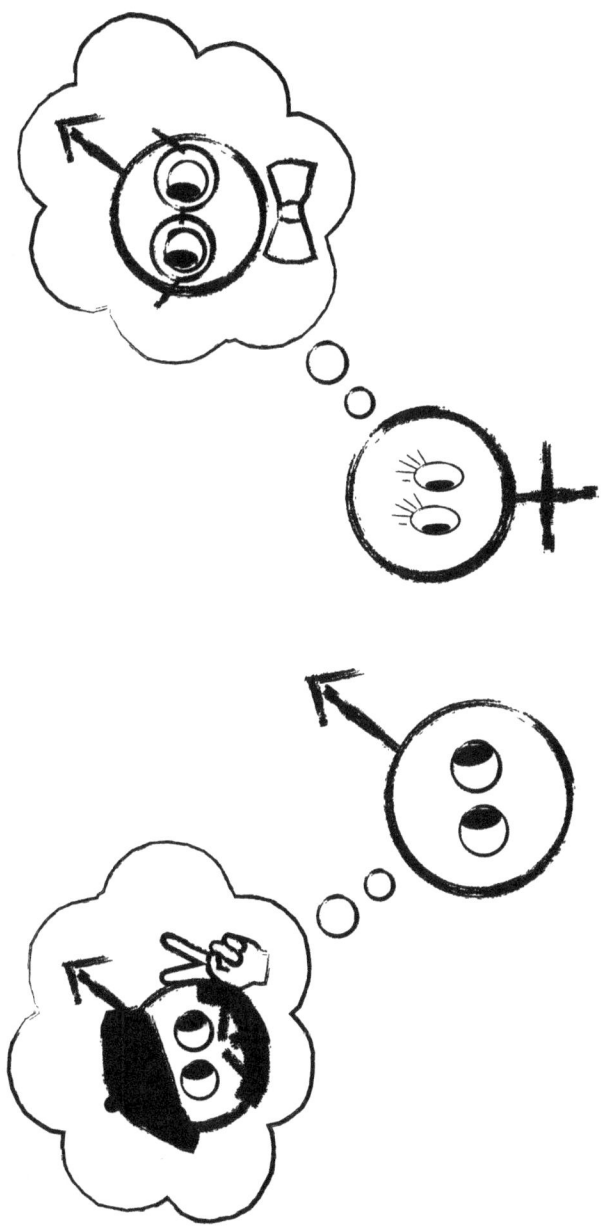

Seriously, we do all need riding mowers.

IT'S IMPORTANT TO HAVE FRIENDS WHO SHARE YOUR LIFE'S AIMS.

WITH AGE COMES A CRAVING FOR SIMPLICITY.

SOME PRACTICAL JOKES WE CAN ONLY DREAM ABOUT.

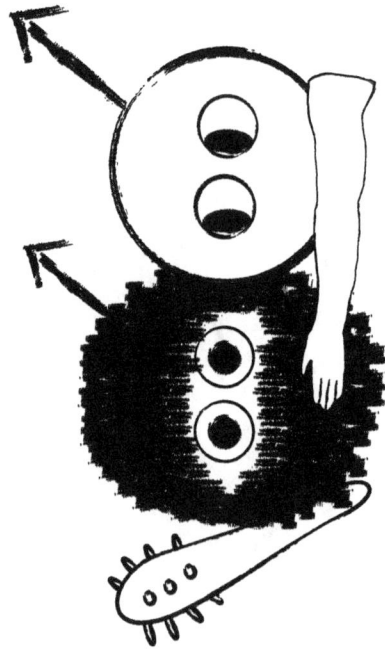

IT'S EMPOWERING TO EMBRACE YOUR INNER WILD MAN.

THE OCCASIONAL CIGAR ISN'T ABOUT THE TOBACCO.

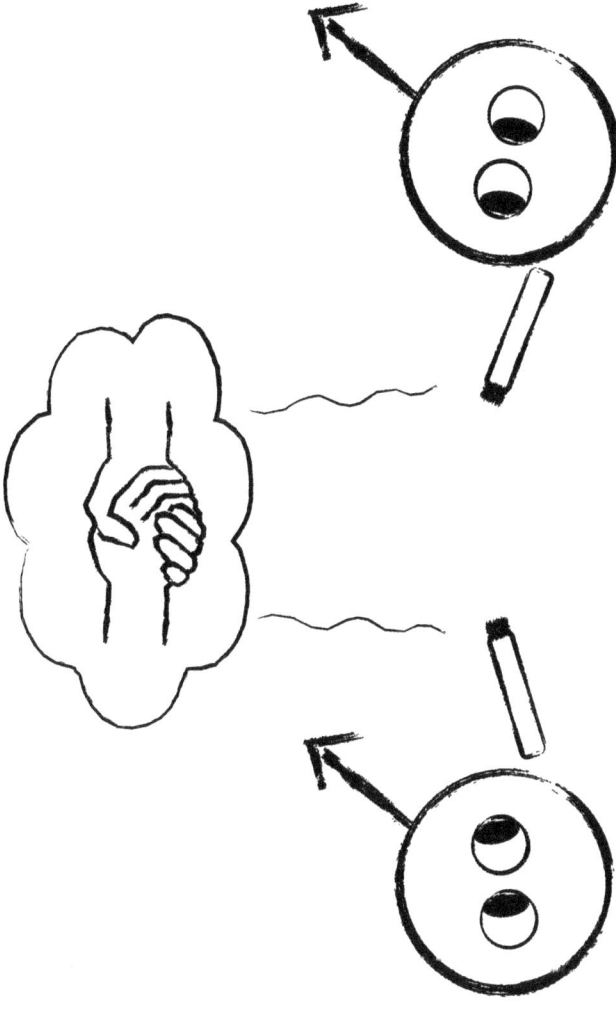

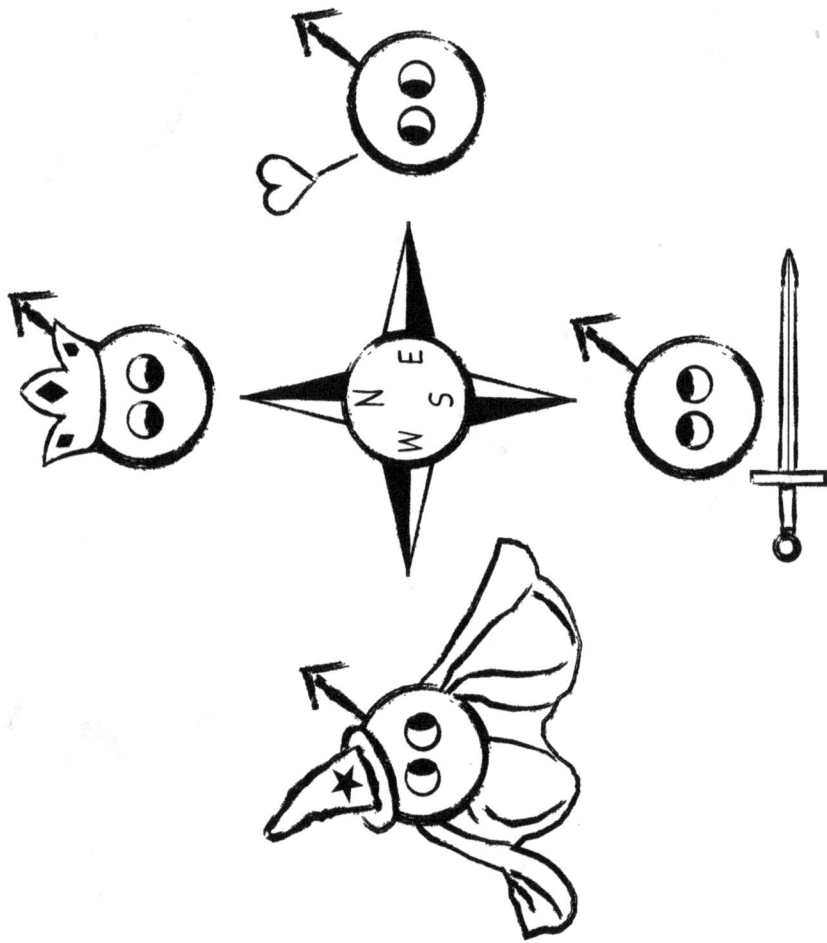

THE MALE ARCHETYPES RESIDE WITHIN EACH OF US.

About the Author

Larry Hughes has been making a living off of the Internet since the word "ecommerce" was considered a typo. But that's just a temporary gig until his audio book "Advanced Karaoke for Mimes" goes viral.

Larry's hobbies include rewording Weird Al Yankovic songs, promoting his custom line of designer bowling socks, and (according to his family) trying way too hard to be funny.

www.ingramcontent.com/pod-product-compliance
Lightning Source LLC
Chambersburg PA
CBHW060707280326
41933CB00012B/2339